Great Estimations

Bruce Goldstone

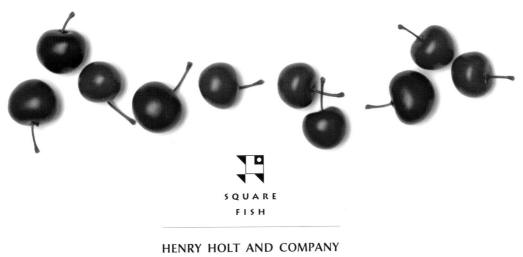

SQUARE
FISH

HENRY HOLT AND COMPANY
NEW YORK

W9-AYA-797

To Melanie,
who I estimate has danced more than 1,500 dances,
eaten more than 4,000 chicken nuggets,
and laughed way more than 25,000 times

There are 2,464 jelly beans in the fishbowl.

SQUARE
FISH
An Imprint of Macmillan

GREAT ESTIMATIONS. Copyright © 2006 by Bruce Goldstone. All rights reserved.
Printed in June 2011 in the United States of America by Worzalla, Stevens Point, Wisconsin.
For information, address Square Fish, 175 Fifth Avenue, New York, NY 10010.

Square Fish and the Square Fish logo are trademarks of Macmillan and
are used by Henry Holt and Company under license from Macmillan.

Photo credits: All images © Arnold and David Katz/Bruce Goldstone with the following exceptions:
pp. 3 and 32, © Michael S. Yamashita/CORBIS; pp. 19 and 20, © John Lund/CORBIS;
p. 25, © Jim Zuckerman/CORBIS; pp. 27 and 28, © Bonnie Muench/CORBIS.

Library of Congress Cataloging-in-Publication Data
Goldstone, Bruce.
Great estimations / Bruce Goldstone.
p.   cm.
ISBN 978-0-312-60887-3
1. Estimation theory—Juvenile literature. I. Title.
QA276.8.G65 2006
519.5'44—dc22
2005019776

Originally published in the United States by Henry Holt and Company
Square Fish logo designed by Filomena Tuosto
First Square Fish Edition: May 2010
Designed by Laurent Linn
10 9 8 7 6 5 4 3
mackids.com

F&P: Q / LEXILE: IG640L

About how many people are swimming in this pool?

Don't count—estimate! An estimate is a good guess. Do you see more than three people? Fewer than 8,000,000?

Those are both estimates, but they are not very accurate. A great estimate is close to the real number. You can train your eyes and your mind to help you make really great estimations.

Estimating can help you get used to working with big numbers. It can help you recognize numbers around you. How many kids are in a marching band? How many whiskers does a cat have? How many windows are in your school building? Practice will help you improve your estimates. Turn the page to get started.

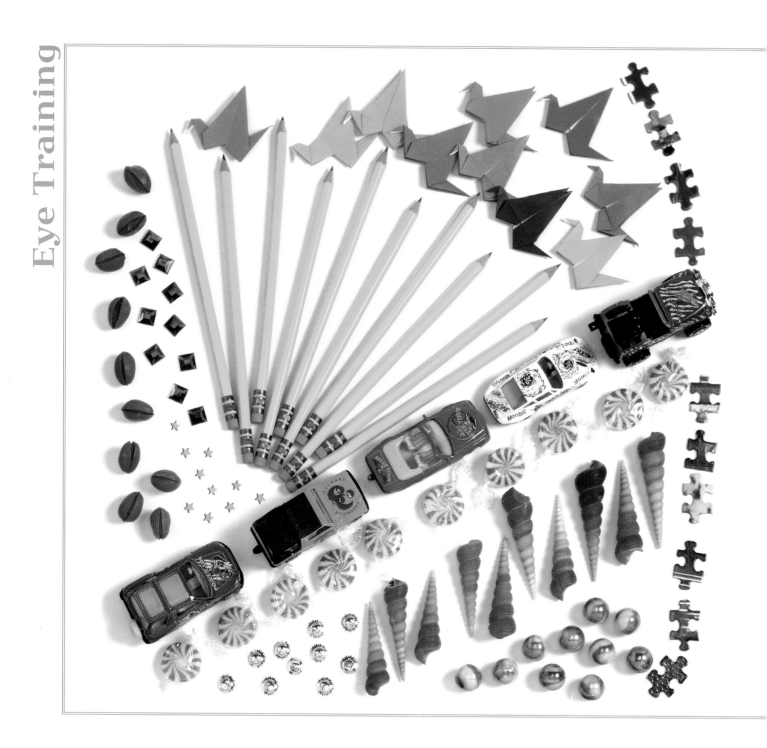

Begin by looking at some tens. What does 10 look like?

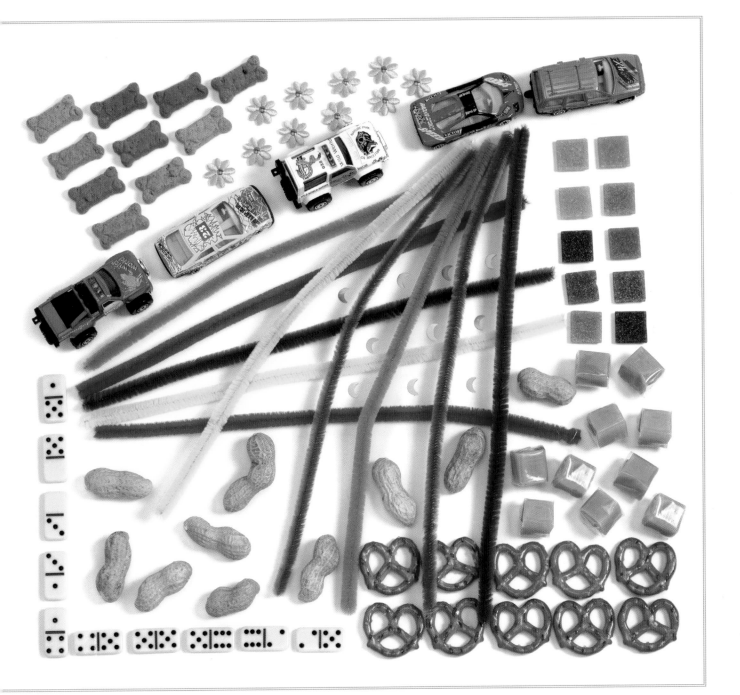

Use these pages for eyeball practice. Train your eye to remember what 10 looks like. You might look at 10 peanuts, 10 pretzels, or 10 pencils. What other tens can you find?

Remember, estimates are not exact answers. Your estimates might be higher or lower than the real numbers. That's fine! Your goal is to come up with a reasonable estimate. That means your estimate is close to the real number.

What does 100 look like?

Hints: Try holding this book upside down. Then, look at these hundreds again. Do they look different upside down? Of course, there are still 100 of each thing. Try looking at things upside down or sideways any time you want a different point of view.

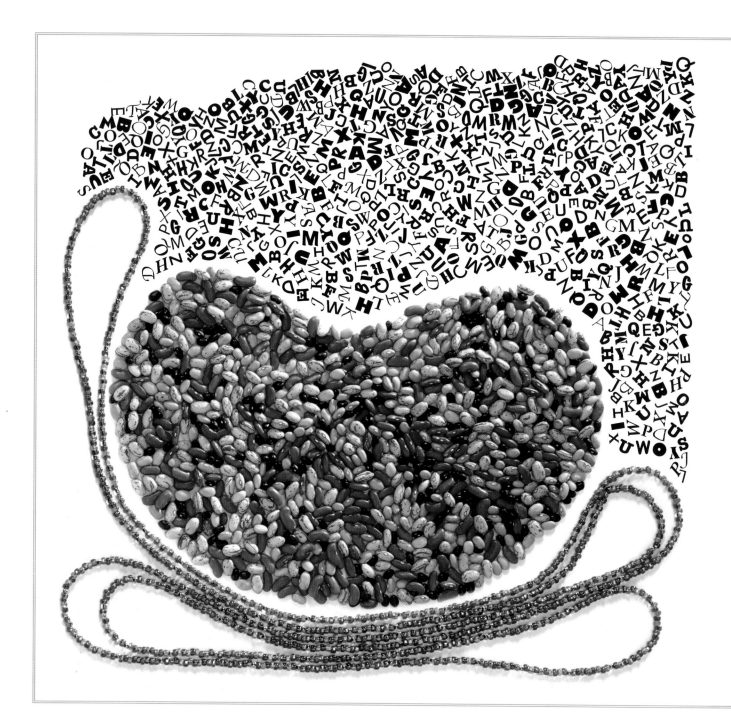

What does 1,000 look like?

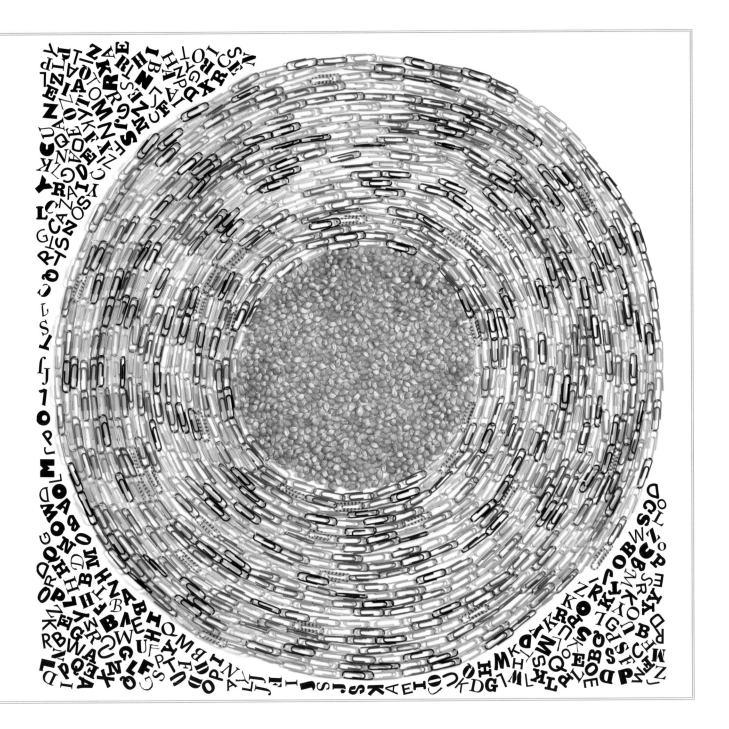

Now compare these thousands to the hundreds. Find groups of ten, too. Count 10 letters or 10 paper clips. Can you cover about 100 beans with your hand? What about 100 beads?

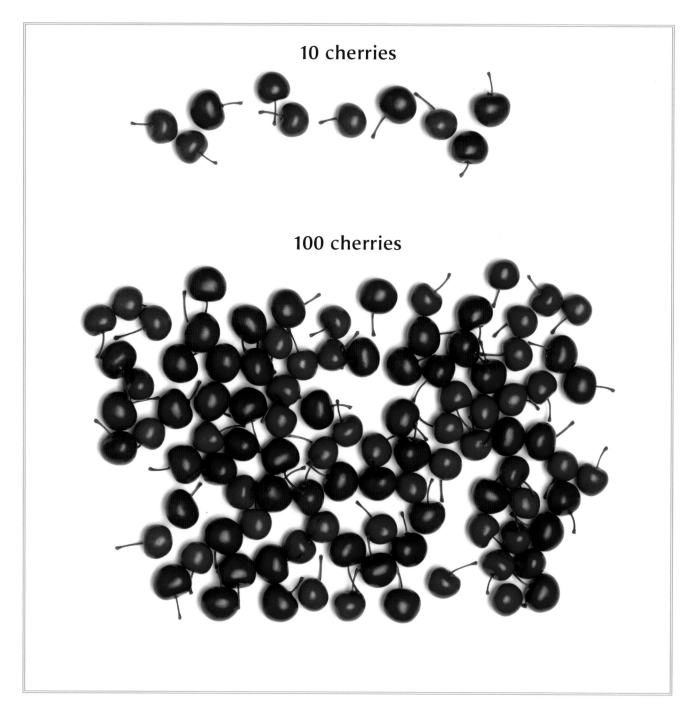

10 cherries

100 cherries

Now that your eyes are trained, let's estimate. Looking at groups can help you estimate. Look at these cherries.

Hints

You can use the groups of cherries as starting places. The pictures of 10 and 100 cherries can help you estimate how many cherries you see on page 11.

About how many cherries are in a quart?

Compare the quart of cherries with the counted cherries. The quart looks like much more than 10 but a little fewer than 100. The estimate could be about 80. What do you think?

100 pennies

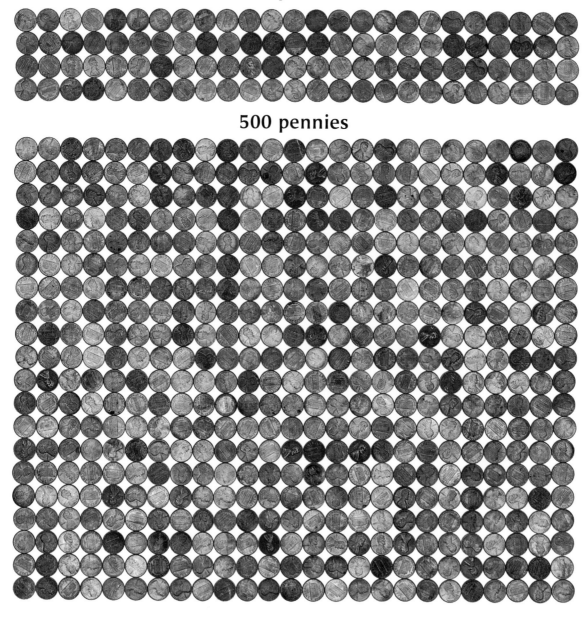

500 pennies

Now look at these groups of pennies. They can help you estimate how many pennies you see on the next page.

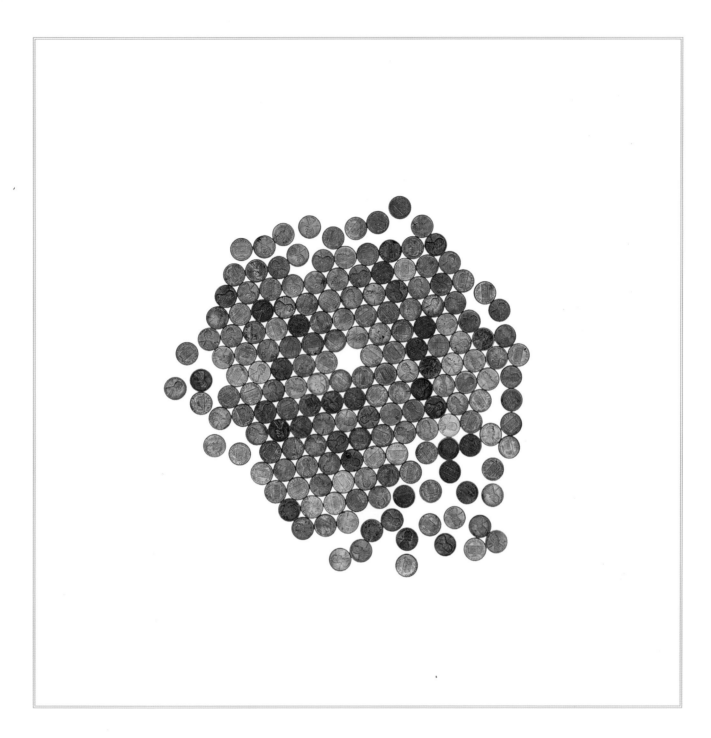

These pennies weigh one pound. About how many pennies do you see?

Hints

You can use the counted pennies to see that there are more than 100 pennies in a pound but fewer than 500. In fact, there are about 182 pennies in a pound. You can use that information to estimate how many pennies you have if you know how much they weigh. Suppose you have a jar of pennies that weighs 15 pounds. Do you think the pennies are worth more than $20? Why or why not?

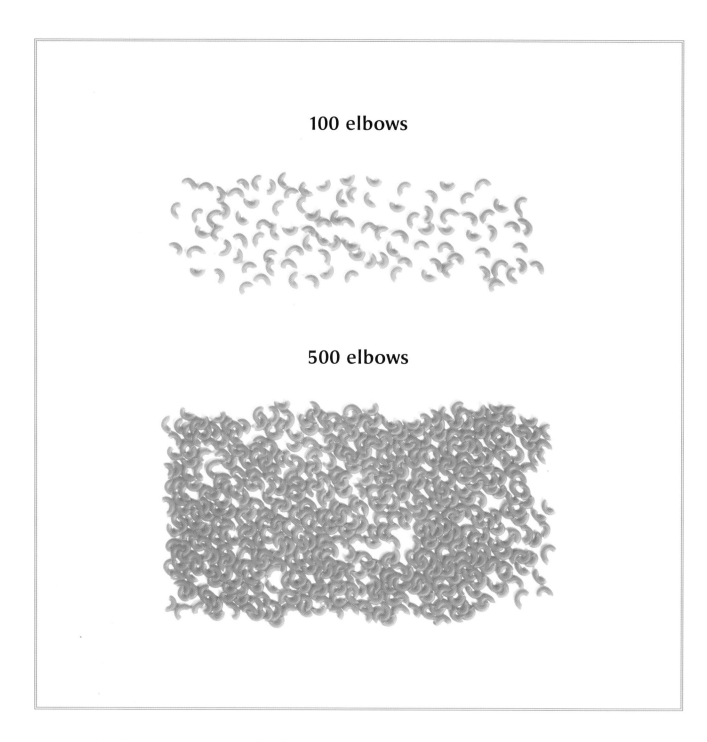

100 elbows

500 elbows

Study these groups of elbow macaroni to help you estimate how many are in a box.

About how many elbows come in a box?

Hints
This photo shows a one-pound box of macaroni. You can see that there are lots more than 500 elbows in the box. Do you think that there are more than 2,000 elbows? Do you think there are more than 5,000?

100 cereal O's

1,000 cereal O's

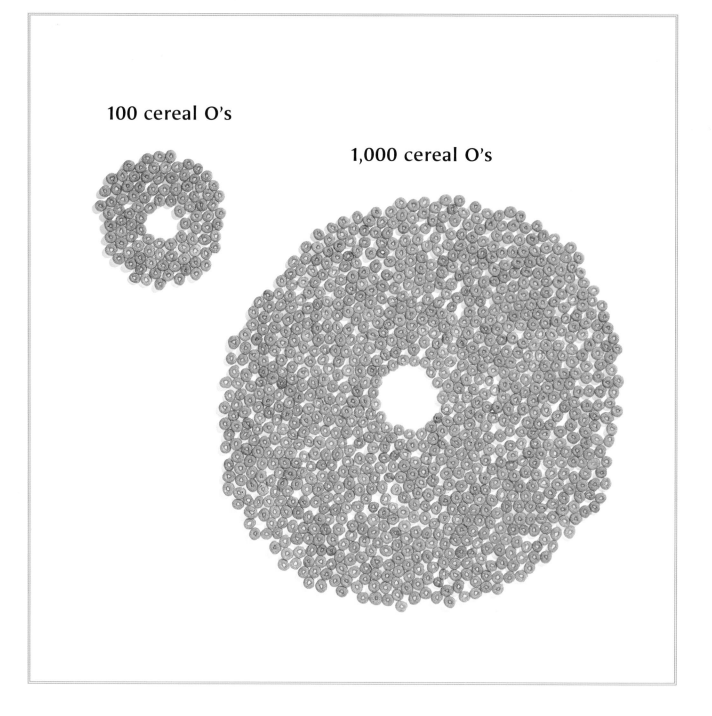

What about cereal? How can you use these groups of O's to help you estimate?

About how many cereal O's do you see?

Hints

This photo shows a box of cereal. You can see that there are lots more than 1,000 cereal O's in the box. Do you think there are more than 8,000 cereal O's?

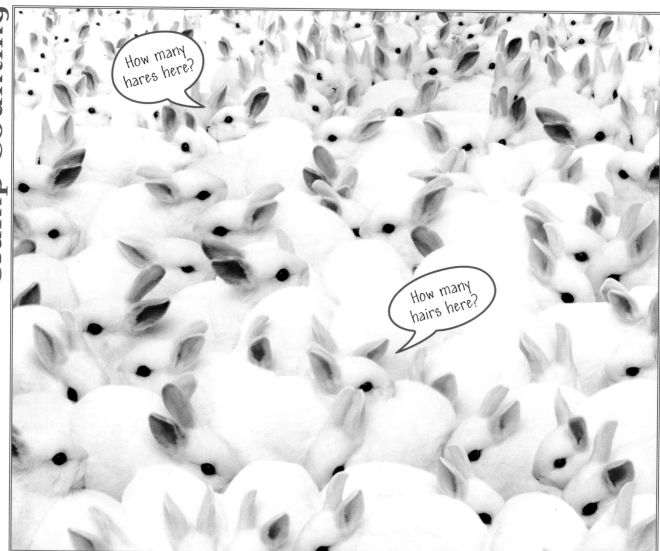

About how many bunnies do you see?

Clump counting can help you to estimate. Start by counting 10 bunnies. Notice how much space 10 bunnies take.

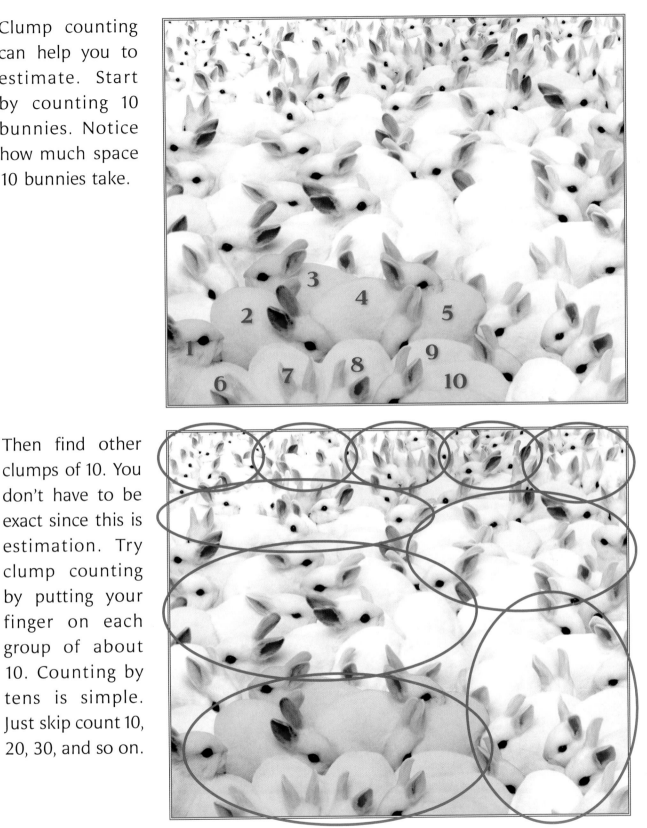

Then find other clumps of 10. You don't have to be exact since this is estimation. Try clump counting by putting your finger on each group of about 10. Counting by tens is simple. Just skip count 10, 20, 30, and so on.

You might count about 10 clumps of 10 bunnies. That makes about 100 bunnies.

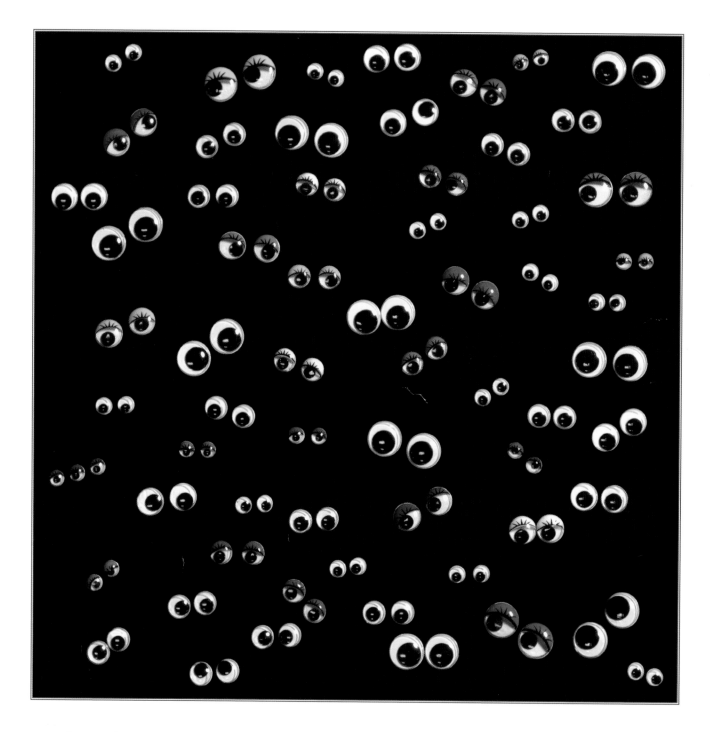

About how many google eyes are looking at you?

Hints

First clump count by tens. Then multiply the number of clumps by 10. Just add 0 to the end of the number. How many clumps did you count? If you counted 12 clumps, add a 0 to the end of 12 to get your estimate—120 google eyes.

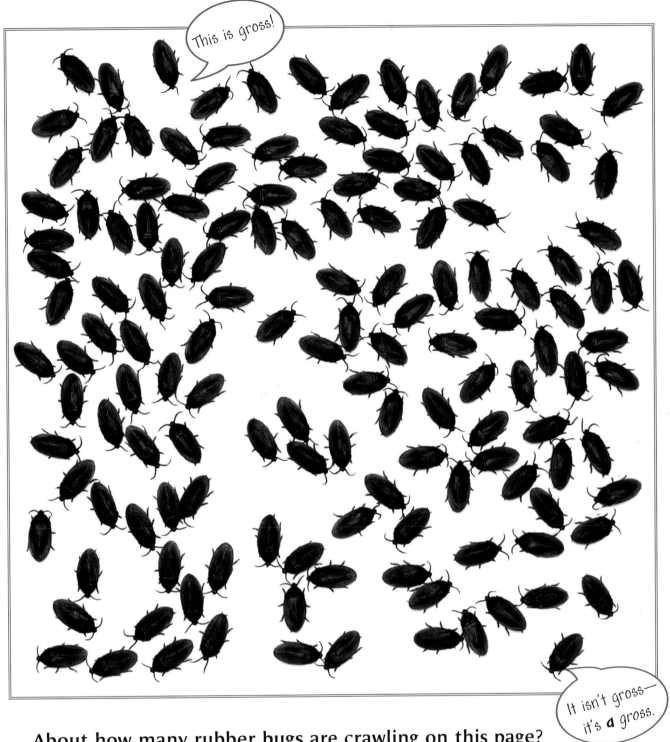

About how many rubber bugs are crawling on this page?

Hints: What is a gross? A gross is a dozen dozen. There are 144 items in a gross. Some things, including novelty toys like rubber bugs, are sold by the gross.

About how many stamps are on this page? About how many dog stamps are there? Do you see more cat stamps?

Hints

Try clump counting by rows. There are 18 rows and about 10 stamps in each row, so there are about 180 stamps. That estimate is a little low because there are more than 10 stamps in every row, so you might round up and say there are about 200 stamps. Are there more cats than dogs? Look for a pattern in the stamps to find the answer.

22 Clump Counting

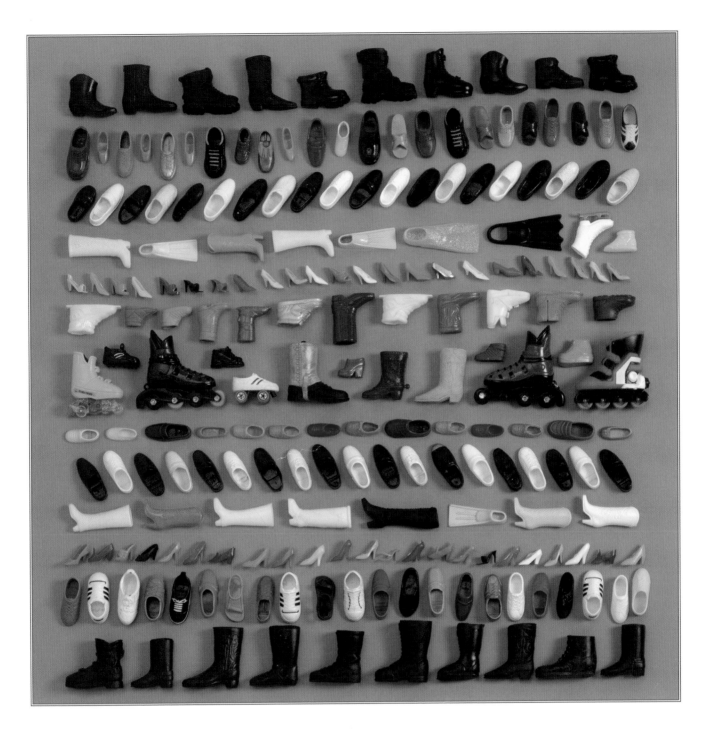

About how many doll shoes do you see?

Hints

You can clump count by different numbers. First clump count shoes by tens. Then try again, but clump count by fives. Remember, you're estimating, so just find about 5 shoes each time as you count 5, 10, 15, 20. Which of your estimates do you think is more accurate? Why?

About how many candies are waiting to be unwrapped?

Try clump counting by twenty-fives to count these candies. Then try clump counting by fifties to count them. You might decide that there are about 50 candies at each end and about 5 groups of 50 in the middle, or 350 sweets in all.

How many spots do these fish have?

You can't see them all, but you can still estimate how many are there.

First estimate the spots you see on one fish. Remember that the fish has two sides, so double your estimate. Then use your estimate to clump count.

Hints

When you estimate, look for numbers that are easy to work with. For example, you might estimate that there are 25 or 28 spots on each side of one fish. You will find that 25 is an easier number to work with. Double 25 to find the number of spots on each fish (remember there are spots on the other side, too). That gives you an estimate of 50 spots per fish. Then clump count by fifties to estimate how many spots these fish have in all. How is your estimate different if you estimate there are 30 spots on one side of one fish?

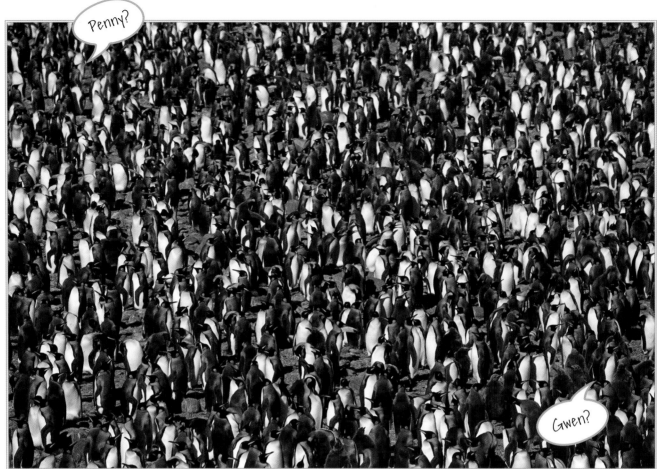

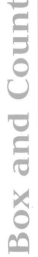

About how many penguins are in this colony?

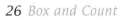

Here's another way to estimate. When lots of things are spread out, you can box and count. Imagine dividing the picture into 100 small boxes.

Then count the things in one box. Choose a box with an average number of penguins.

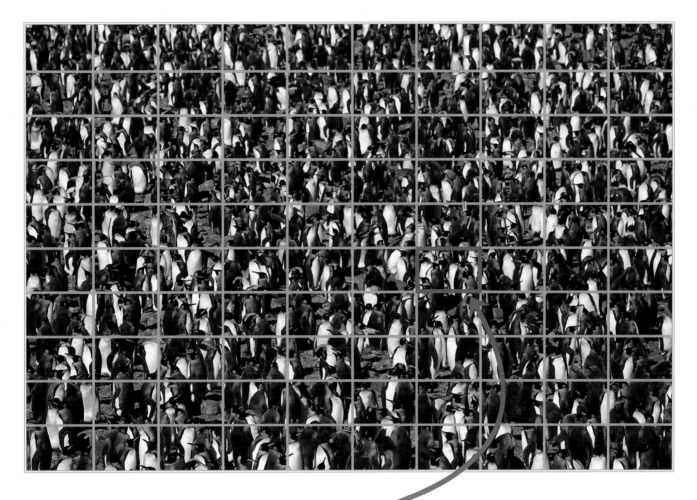

There are about 12 penguins in this box.

Multiply the number by 100 boxes to get your estimate. It's easy to multiply by 100—just add two 0's to the end of the number. So add two 0's to 12 and you get the estimate of 1,200. That's a good estimate for the total number of penguins.

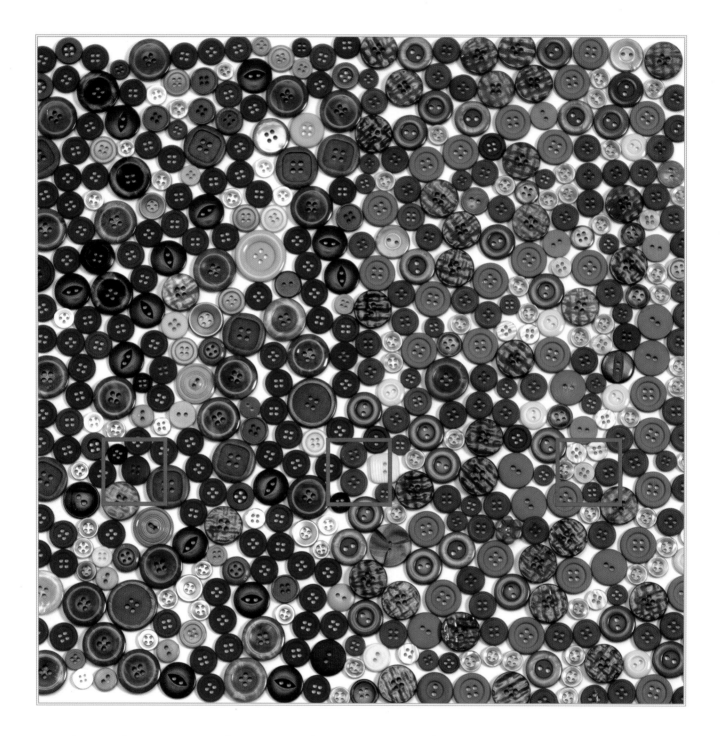

About how many buttons do you see? About how many of them are green?

Hints

About how many buttons do you see in the boxes? Look inside one box. You see some whole buttons and some button parts. You can estimate that there are about 7 buttons in each box. Multiply by 100 to get your estimate: 700 buttons. About half of them are green, so you can estimate that there are 350 green buttons.

About how many grains of rice do you see?

Hints You might estimate that you see about 150 grains of rice in the small box. The box is $\frac{1}{100}$ of the picture, so multiply your estimate by 100. To find your estimate, add two 0's to the end and get 15,000. That is a good estimate for all the grains of rice you see on this page.

How will you estimate these jelly beans? You might try clump counting or box and count. It's up to you.

Hints Your eyes can help you estimate, too. Do you see more than 100 jelly beans? More than 1,000? You might compare these jelly beans to some of the other things you have already estimated.

How many jelly beans are crowded in this fishbowl?

Remember, there are lots of jelly beans that you can't see in the middle of the bowl.

Here's one way you can estimate. First estimate how many jelly beans you see in the front layer of the bowl. Then estimate how many layers there are. If you estimate 10 layers, just add a 0 to the end of your number.

Hints You might estimate that you can see about 250 jelly beans in the front of the bowl. If there are 10 layers of beans, there are about 2,500 jelly beans inside. (But if you want to know the exact number, it's hidden somewhere in this book. Can you find it?)

It's time to dive back into the pool! About how many swimmers do you see now?

Now that you've gotten your feet wet, keep estimating wherever you go. You'll find great estimation puzzles everywhere you look. Here are just a few to get you started.

About how many . . .

   . . . people are in line in front of you at the amusement park?

   . . . seats are in your school bus?

   . . . petals are on a flower?

   . . . hairs are on a cat?

   . . . people are in a parade?

   . . . words are in this book?

Hints

To count swimmers, try clump counting by tens or twenty-fives. Or just use your sense of what 100 looks like to make an estimate. Are there are about 250 people in this pool?

   When you are estimating things in the real world, ask a friend to estimate, too. Then compare your numbers and talk about big differences. You might think there are about 700 tiles in that mosaic while your friend thinks there are about 7,000. Talk it over to see which estimate is more reasonable. Just remember, you don't need to count every piece to make great estimations!